I0402966

notebook
- This notebook belongs to -

Copyright© 2019 Jocs Press

All rights reserved and protected under the copyright, designs, and patents act 1988.

www.BrandingbyJuls.com

Print on demand by Amazon

No part of this book may be reproduced, stored in a retrieval system, transmitted in any form or used in any manner (photocopying or scanning) without express permission from the author and copyright owner. Do not attempt to share, copy or replicate this material as this is illegal.

First edition.

Follow **@jocspress** and **@brandingbyjuls** on Instagram | Facebook | Pinterest

THOUGHTS & IDEAS

THOUGHTS & IDEAS

THOUGHTS & IDEAS

THOUGHTS & IDEAS

THOUGHTS & IDEAS

THOUGHTS & IDEAS

THOUGHTS & IDEAS

THOUGHTS & IDEAS

THOUGHTS & IDEAS

THOUGHTS & IDEAS

THOUGHTS & IDEAS

THOUGHTS & IDEAS

THOUGHTS & IDEAS

THOUGHTS & IDEAS

THOUGHTS & IDEAS

THOUGHTS & IDEAS

THOUGHTS & IDEAS

THOUGHTS & IDEAS

THOUGHTS & IDEAS

THOUGHTS & IDEAS

THOUGHTS & IDEAS

THOUGHTS & IDEAS

THOUGHTS & IDEAS

THOUGHTS & IDEAS

THOUGHTS & IDEAS

THOUGHTS & IDEAS

THOUGHTS & IDEAS

THOUGHTS & IDEAS

THOUGHTS & IDEAS

THOUGHTS & IDEAS

THOUGHTS & IDEAS

THOUGHTS & IDEAS

THOUGHTS & IDEAS

THOUGHTS & IDEAS

THOUGHTS & IDEAS

THOUGHTS & IDEAS

THOUGHTS & IDEAS

THOUGHTS & IDEAS

THOUGHTS & IDEAS

THOUGHTS & IDEAS

THOUGHTS & IDEAS

THOUGHTS & IDEAS

THOUGHTS & IDEAS

THOUGHTS & IDEAS

THOUGHTS & IDEAS

THOUGHTS & IDEAS

THOUGHTS & IDEAS

THOUGHTS & IDEAS

THOUGHTS & IDEAS

THOUGHTS & IDEAS

THOUGHTS & IDEAS

THOUGHTS & IDEAS

THOUGHTS & IDEAS

THOUGHTS & IDEAS

THOUGHTS & IDEAS

THOUGHTS & IDEAS

THOUGHTS & IDEAS

THOUGHTS & IDEAS

www.ingramcontent.com/pod-product-compliance
Lightning Source LLC
Chambersburg PA
CBHW081654220526
45466CB00009B/2755